#6 in the Molly Learns Series

Molly Learns 10 Facts About Ulysses S. Grant

By Marla Harms Judge
and Molly the History Dog

I0100312

I pose and smile with a living history interpreter portraying Ulysses S. Grant!

Book design by
Maria Loysa-Bel Nueve-de los Angeles

ISBN Paperback 978-1-965334-42-3
ISBN Hardcover 978-1-965334-41-6

Library of Congress Control Number: 2025916650

Please write to us at:
Mollythehistorydog@gmail.com
Visit: mollythehistorydog.com

CRIPPLED BEAGLE PUBLISHING

Crippled Beagle Publishing, Knoxville, TN, USA
crippledbeaglepublishing.com

Our love and thanks to everyone
that helped us create our book!
... especially RGJ!

Molly and General Grant

Let Us have peace.

Ulysses S. Grant

Hello! My name is Molly.
I am a dalmatian dog.
I am white with many black spots.
Did you know that dalmatians are born pure white?
We don't start getting our spots until we are
about 3-4 weeks old.

Newborn puppies and puppies about 8 weeks old snuggle as they grow.

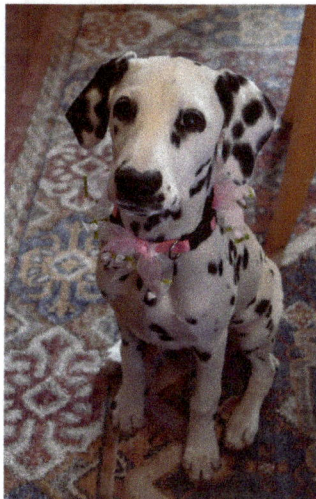

Me, Molly, when I was just a baby!

I stand guard with a hat similar to what Ulysses S. Grant may have worn when he was a general.

Ulysses S. Grant
This portrait was painted when he was president.

You may have noticed that I am called
MOLLY THE HISTORY DOG.
That is because my human family and I
love to travel and learn about history.

At last count we have visited 32 states.
We visit national park sites whenever we can.

Some sites protect nature.
Some sites protect our country's history.
Have you ever visited a national park?
What was your favorite area?
I think the Grand Canyon is pretty amazing!

Have you guessed who
we are going to
learn about in this book?

He was both a general
in the army
and a president
of the United States!

We call him
Ulysses S. Grant.
But as you will learn in
our book, there is an interesting
story about his name.

Ulysses was an important man
in our country's history.
Let's learn about him!

Ulysses' story began on
April 27, 1822.
He was born in Point Pleasant, Ohio.
Ulysses was the oldest of six children.

April 1822

Sunday	Monday	Tuesday	Wednesday	Thursday	Friday	Saturday
	1	2	3	4	5	6
7	8	9	10	11	12	13
14	15	16	17	18	19	20
21	22	23	24	25	26	27
28	29	30				

His father was Jesse Grant.
His mother was Hannah Simpson Grant

Jesse Grant

Hannah Simpson Grant

He lived in this house until he was
almost one year old.

Ulysses Grant birthplace.

When he was born,
his parents named him
Hiram Ulysses Grant.
As he grew up, his family
and friends called him Lys.

A young living historian portrays Ulysses as a boy.

Since Ulysses had brothers and sisters,
he always had someone to play with as he grew up.
Do you have brothers or sisters to play with?
What kind of games do you think the
children played when Ulysses was a boy?

Remember, they did not have
TVs or computer games back then.
Do you have a favorite game?
I like to play fetch! I love to run!
When the weather was warm and
the children could play outside,
they played games like hopscotch,
rolling a hoop, and marbles.

Boys playing a game of marbles and girls playing with rolling hoops.

A young boy fishes.

Ulysses loved to fish and ride his horse.

Would you like to hear a funny story
I learned about Ulysses
when he was a young boy?
One time, a circus came to town.
The ringmaster offered 5 dollars to
anyone who could ride their pony.
Five dollars was a lot of money to Ulysses!

Many of Ulysses' friends tried to ride
the pony but failed. Ulysses mounted
the pony, and no matter what the pony did,
Ulysses held on!
To try to get him to fall off, the
ringmaster had a monkey jump onto
the pony behind Ulysses.
But still, Ulysses rode the pony!
Finally, the ringmaster had to
pay Ulysses the money.

Have you ever been to a circus?
I think I would like to go sometime.

When the weather was bad and
cold outside, the family played checkers
and a game called Fox and Geese.

The Fox and Geese game was a marble game.

In the winter Ulysses enjoyed ice skating.
One time he stayed outside skating for so long
that his feet were frozen when he got home!
Thinking about that makes my paws ache.
Do you like to play outside in the winter?
I do! I love to chase snowballs.

As you can tell, Ulysses loved
to spend time outside.
He would spend time fishing and riding
his horse every chance he got.
Ulysses began riding at a very young age.
As a young man he became known
as a skilled trainer. His mother said,
"Horses seem to understand Ulysses."

This sketch illustrates Ulysses showing off his trick riding skills.

Would you like to hear the story of how
Hiram Ulysses Grant became Ulysses S. Grant?
When Ulysses was a young man, he left his
family to attend West Point Military Academy.
He was not sure he wanted to be a soldier,
but his father insisted he go.
When he arrived at school, he discovered
that someone had mistakenly
registered him as Ulysses S. Grant.
Instead of trying to fix the error,
he continued to use the name
for the rest of his life.

A soldier salutes his commanding officer at West Point.

I was not surprised to learn that while at West Point, Ulysses excelled in horseback riding.

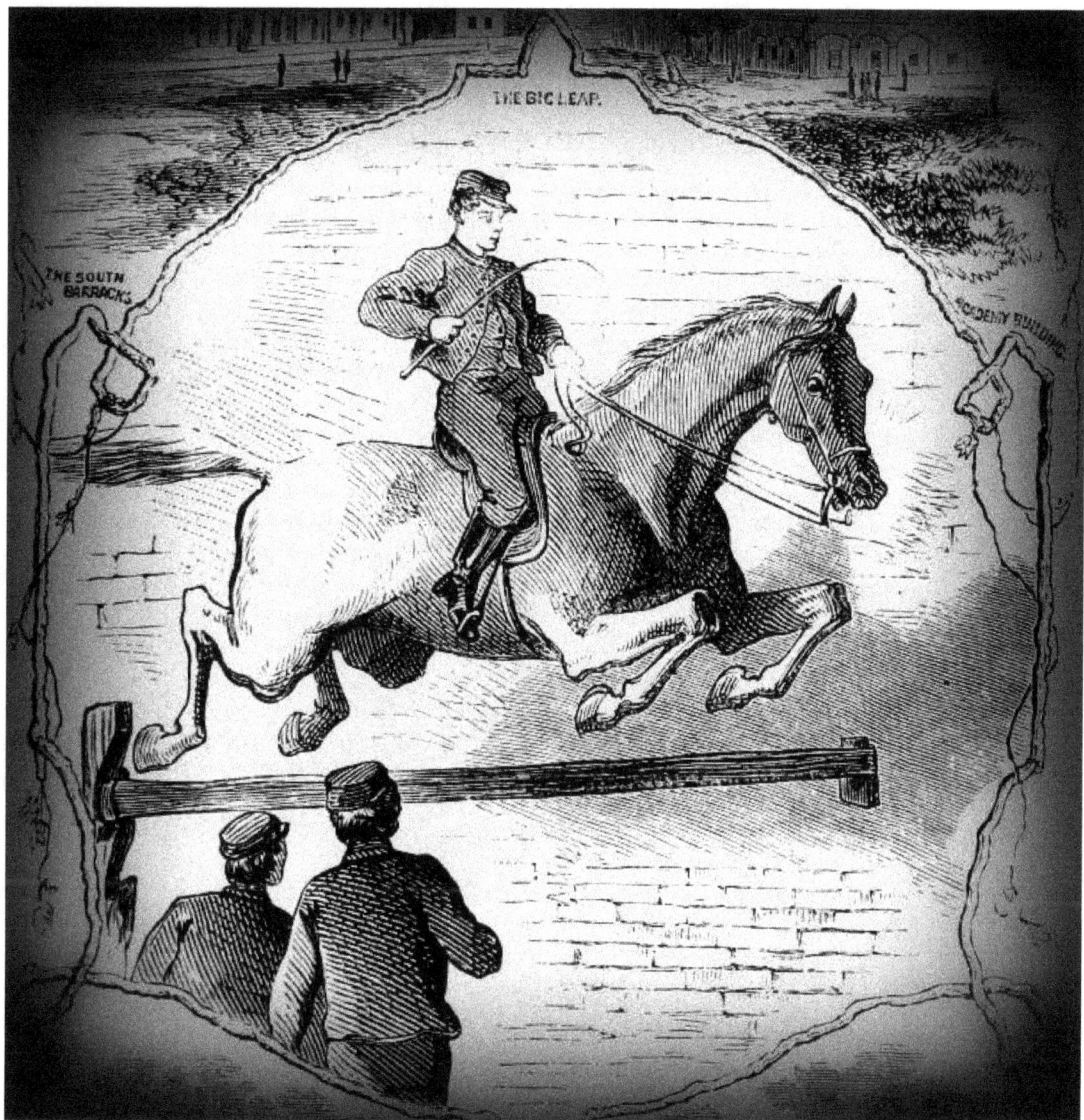

This sketch depicts Ulysses riding at West Point.

I was excited to visit a stable a while back.
I got to meet many beautiful horses.
This is one of the horses that I met.
Her name is Cookie!
Have you ever ridden a horse?
I think it would be fun.

Cookie the horse was fun to visit!

When I visited the stable, I made a new friend named Emma. One of Emma's jobs is to groom Cookie. I learned that brushing and cleaning a horse is called *grooming!*

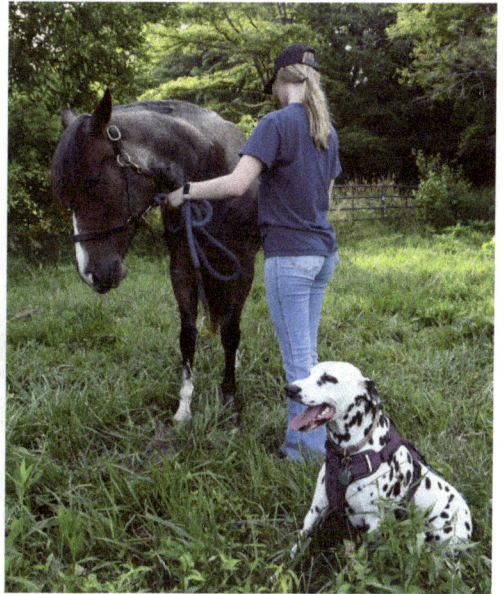

Emma, Cookie and Molly

I like to be brushed, and I bet
it feels good to Cookie too!
I think I understand why Ulysses
liked horses so much.
They are neat!

Riding horses was not the only talent
Ulysses had at West Point.
He loved to draw and paint.
A few of his pictures can still be seen today.
Do you like to create art?
Do you draw, paint, sew, or build?
It is fun to be creative!

This is a sketch drawn by Ulysses.

While Ulysses was at West Point, he
was given a nickname that followed
him the rest of his life.
His classmates called him Sam.
Do you have a nickname?
Many famous people have
nicknames, too.
In our other books we learned that
Abraham Lincoln was called "Abe."
(A name he did not like!)
President Lincoln's nickname for
his wife Mary was "Molly." (I like that!)
President Washington is often called
"The Father of Our Country."
Theordore Roosevelt is often called "Teddy."

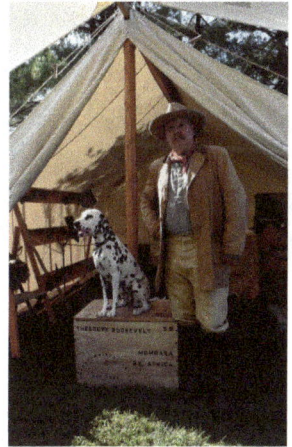

In these pictures, I pose with Mr. and Mrs. Lincoln, General Washington
and Theodore Roosevelt

After Ulysses graduated from West Point,
he was sent to an army post in Missouri
called Jefferson Barracks.
It is near St. Louis, Missouri, and
that is where he met his wife.
A fellow soldier named Fredrick Dent
invited Ulysses to visit his family's home,
called White Haven.

I visit White Haven and have my picture taken!

Ulysses fell in love with Fredrick's sister, Julia.
Ulysses and Julie got married and raised
a family of three sons and one daughter.

Mrs. Julia Grant

Ulysses thought Julia was a very beautiful
woman, but Julia was always self-
conscious about the way she looked.
Julia had a health condition that caused
her eyes not to look straight ahead.
This did not matter at all to Ulysses!
I agree with him.
Having a physical challenge does not
make anyone less beautiful.

The Grant family

The Grants named their first son after
his uncle who introduced them.
He was called Fredrick Dent Grant.
Their second son was named after his
father, Ulysses S. Grant Jr.
That son's nickname was Buck.
Their daughter was named Ellen
Wrenshall Grant. They called her Nellie.
Their youngest son was called
Jesse Root Grant II.
He was named for his grandfather.

Ulysses and Julia loved their children
very much. He missed them a great
deal whenever he had to be away
while serving in the army.
When it was possible, he would have
Julia and the children join him.

Know what makes me happy?
Ulysses loved his horses, and his DOGS!
At White Haven, the Grants had
a newfoundland dog named Leo.
Newfoundlands are huge and
sometimes as tall as ponies.
Leo's job was to help the cook
catch chickens for supper!

A newfoundland dog

When the Grants moved into the
White House after Ulysses became
president, they brought along
another newfoundland
dog named Faithful.
Faithful actually belonged to
Ulysses' son, Jesse.
They had many adventures
while living in the White House.

Do you ever wonder what kind of food Ulysses liked to eat?
I like to eat candy!
But it is bad for me, so I usually have dog food and dog treats.
What do you like to eat?
Ulysses liked to eat something called rice pudding.
I think it looks kind of yucky!
What do you think?

Rice Pudding

In case you would like to try
making rice pudding, I found a recipe for you.
Be sure to ask an adult for permission
and help before you start.

RICE PUDDING

You will need the following ingredients:

1 ½ cups of cold water

¾ cup uncooked white rice

2 cups milk

1/3 cup white sugar

¼ teaspoon salt

1 large egg, beaten

(To make a beaten egg, just put it in a cup and use a fork to mix it up!)

2/3 cup golden raisins

1 tablespoon butter

½ teaspoon vanilla extract

a sprinkle of cinnamon

First - Pour the water into a pot. Bring it to a boil. Add the rice. Turn the heat down low. Cover the pot. Let it cook until all the water is gone—about 20 minutes.

Second – In a new pot, add the cooked rice, 1 ½ cups of milk, sugar, and salt. Cook over medium heat. Stir often until it's thick and creamy—about 15 minutes.

Third– Add more milk, the beaten egg, and raisins. Cook for 2 more minutes, stirring all the time.

Fourth– Take the pot off the heat. Add butter and a little more salt. Sprinkle cinnamon sticks on top.

Serve warm—and enjoy!
This recipe makes enough for 4 people.

Ulysses served in the army for many years.
When he had to be away from his family,
he missed them terribly.
Eventually, he decided that the army
was not for him anymore.
He left the army and moved his family
to St. Louis, Missouri, to be near Julia's family.
Later, they moved to Galena, Illinois,
near Ulysses' family.

When they lived in St. Louis they
had a small farm that Ulysses
named "Hard Scrabble."

Hard Scrabble

In 1861, the United States began
fighting what is called the Civil War.
Ulysses rejoined the army to help keep the
United States together as one country.
In 1864, President Lincoln asked
Ulysses to become the general
in charge of the army.
This was a great honor!

General Grant

During the war, Ulysses led his
soldiers into many battles.
He was proud to be the general
in charge, but it made him sad when
soldiers were hurt or killed in battle.

During the war, Ulysses often rode his favorite horse named Cincinnati.

After the war, the people of the town of Galena, Ilinois, gave a house to the Grant family as a gift.

I visited the house and had my picture taken!

When the war was over, people thought that, since Ulysses had been such a fine general, he would make a good president! In 1869, he became the 18th President of the United States. He was president for 8 years.

When Ulysses finished his time as
president, he and Julia traveled around
the world for over two years.
They visited many interesting places.

They began their journey in Liverpool, England.
They met the Queen of England, Victoria.

Victoria was the queen in England for more than 63 years!

They traveled to France, Ireland, and
several other countries in Europe.

They went to Egypt, India, and China.
In Japan, they met Emperor Meiji and his family.

Emperor Meiji and family

When the Grants returned to the
United States, they made their
home in New York City.

Ulysses wrote a book about his life.
He wanted people to know about
all the things he had done.

The Grant Family

Hiram Ulysses Grant
Lys
Ulysses S. Grant
General Grant
Sam
President Grant

There were many names through the years for this interesting and accomplished man!

I hope you have enjoyed learning
10 facts about Ulysses S. Grant.

These are some of the facts we talked about:

1. When and where Ulysses was born.
2. The story of Ulysses' name.
3. Ulysses was in the army and a general.
4. We learned about Ulysses' family.
5. The Grants had a home called Hard Scrabble.
6. We learned Ulysses liked to draw.
7. Ulysses liked to eat rice pudding.
8. Ulysses liked horses and dogs!
9. After being president, the Grants traveled.
10. Ulysses wrote a book about his life.

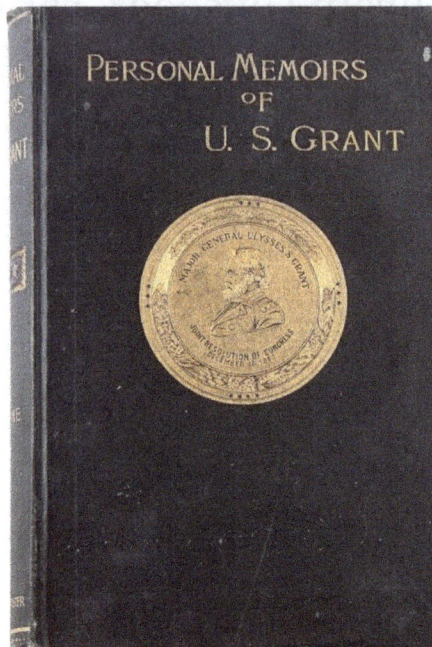

Would you like to color a picture of Ulysses S. Grant?

Color a picture of President Grant!

Would you like to do a crossword puzzle about what you learned in our book?

Name:_____

Ulysses S. Grant
Complete the crossword puzzle below

Created using the crossword maker
on TheTeachersCorner.net

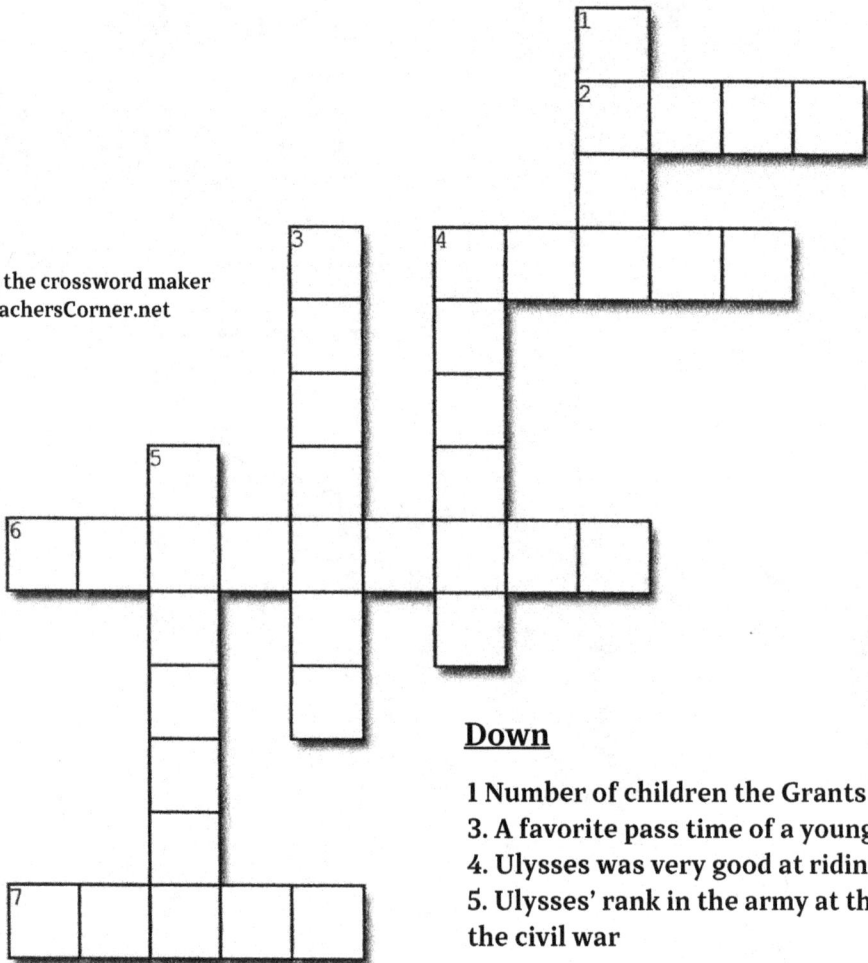

Down

1 Number of children the Grants had
3. A favorite pass time of a young Ulysses
4. Ulysses was very good at riding ___
5. Ulysses' rank in the army at the end of the civil war

Across

2. State Ulysses was born in
4. Ulysses' first name when he was born
6. Ulysses was the 18th ___
7. Mrs. Grant's first name

(You can find the answers on the next page)

38

Crossword puzzle answers

Across
2 – OHIO
4 – HIRAM
6 – PRESIDENT
7 – JULIA

Down
1 – FOUR
3 – FISHING
4 – HORSES
5 – GENERAL

Meet the authors!

Molly is an amazing dalmatian.
She loves to travel and visit new places.
When home, she loves to run and
play in the yard with her little brother, Murphy.
(Murphy is a dalmatian too, but he has *brown* spots.)

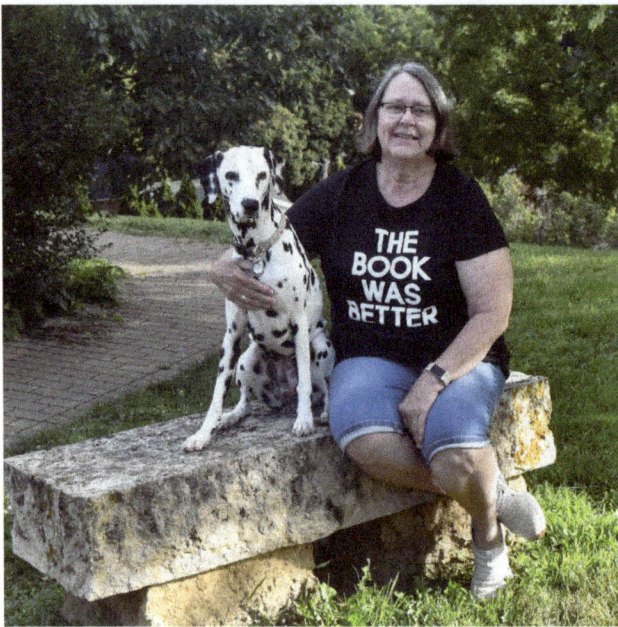

Molly and Marla at Grant's Home in Galena, Il.

Marla is a history nerd!
She loves to help people learn about history.
Marla has worked as a school librarian,
a park ranger and a living history interpreter.
History is fun!

Thank you to the living history interpreters
who posed for photos in our book.

William Golladay
Samuel Golladay
Lillian Shafer
Rose Hoehnle
Larry Werline – General and President Grant
Thanks to Libbie South for allowing
Pepto Metallic Chic aka Cookie to be in our book
Emma Mendenhall (Cookie's groom)
Sister Haven Ranch – Susan and Helena Rosse,
for allowing us to take photos at their stable

Photo Credits
Marla Judge
Opening page, Thank you page
1, 2, 4, 8, 9, 11, 17, 19, 20, 28, 31, 40
Libbie South - 16
Public Domain
Dove, 1, 7, 10, 11, 12, 13, 14, 15, 21,
22, 24, 25, 26, 37
National Park Service
9, 18, 19, 29, 36
Library of Congress
3, 7, 9, 16, 31, 32, 33, 34
Smithsonian
21, 30, 35

There are several places you can
visit to learn more about the Grants.

Ulysses S. Grant National Historic Site
7400 Grant Rd.
St. Louis, Missouri 63123
National Park Service

Grant's Home
500 Bouthillier St.
Galena, Ilinois 61036
www.granthome.org

Grant Cottage State Historic Site
1000 Mt. McGregor Rd
Wilton, New York 12831
www.grantcottage.org

U.S. Grant Birthplace
15510St. Rte. 2325
Moscow, Ohio 45153

General Grant National Memorial
(Grant's Tomb)
W 122nd St &, Riverside Dr
New York, New York 10027
National Park Service

Other books in the *Molly Learns Series*

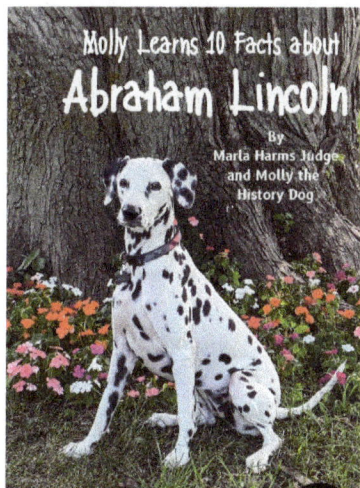

Molly Learns 10 Facts about **Abraham Lincoln** By Marla Harms Judge and Molly the History Dog

FIRST OF THE SERIES!

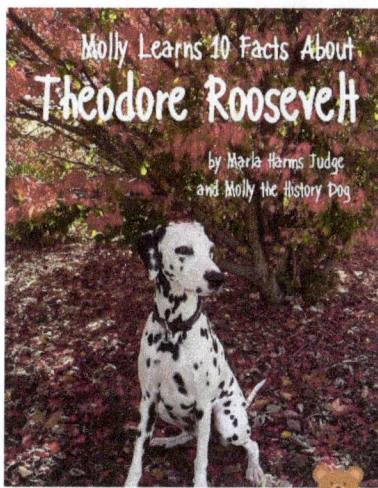

Molly Learns 10 Facts About **Theodore Roosevelt** by Marla Harms Judge and Molly the History Dog

Second in the Molly Learns Series

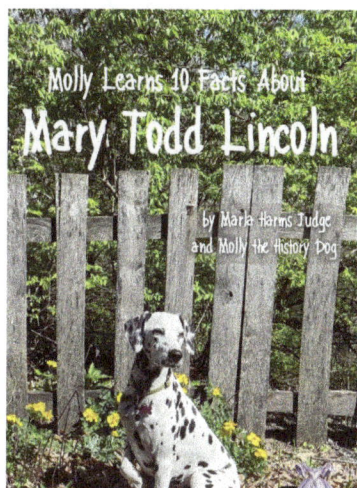

Molly Learns 10 Facts About **Mary Todd Lincoln** by Marla Harms Judge and Molly the History Dog

Third in the Molly Learns Series

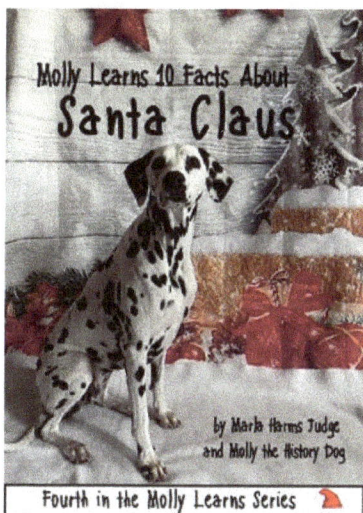

Molly Learns 10 Facts About **Santa Claus** by Marla Harms Judge and Molly the History Dog

Fourth in the Molly Learns Series

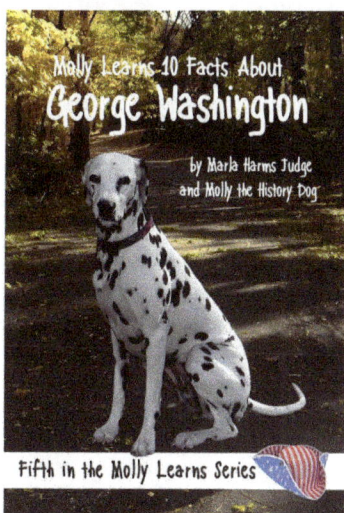

Molly Learns 10 Facts About **George Washington** by Marla Harms Judge and Molly the History Dog

Fifth in the Molly Learns Series

Available at: CRIPPLED BEAGLE PUBLISHING   amazon   BARNES&NOBLE

Visit us at mollythehistorydog.com
and on Facebook: Molly the History Dog.

www.ingramcontent.com/pod-product-compliance
Lightning Source LLC
Chambersburg PA
CBHW061754260326
41914CB00006B/1098